# In the night sky

**i-SPY**

D0278062

# INTRODUCTION

To appreciate the sky and stars in their full glory you need to find the best possible conditions, preferably somewhere really dark, maybe at the bottom of your garden. You will get good views during long winter nights but, if you live in a town, the glare from the lights may make it difficult to see very faint stars. You can see most when you are in the country or at the seaside so try watching the stars when you are on holiday. There are three things you should remember: Always tell your parents if you want to watch the stars. Astronomy is a good excuse for staying up late! Try to get your parents or an elder brother or sister to come with you. Always wear warm clothes. Even in the summer, it is sometimes very cold at night and, if you shiver, it wobbles your binoculars or telescope! Because you are out in the dark, you need a torch to see your book. A bright light dazzles your eyes, so cover the end of the torch with red tissue paper or red plastic film to give a dim red light. After you have been outside for a while you will find you can see much more than at first as your eyes become more accustomed to the dark.

## How to use your i-SPY book

You will need 1000 points to send off for your i-SPY certificate (see page 64) but that is not too difficult because there are masses of points in every book. Each entry has a star or circle and points value beside it. The stars represent harder to spot entries. As you make each i-SPY, write your score in the circle or star and where there is a question, check your answer against the correct one on page 63.

When the Moon (especially the Full Moon) is low on the horizon it appears enormous. In fact, it is actually exactly the same size as when it is high in the sky. This is known as the 'Moon Illusion' – your brain simply thinks it is bigger when compared with distant hills or buildings. Test it for yourself: hold a finger at arm's length and you will see that it is about twice the width of the Moon, wherever the Moon is in the sky. Actually, the same effect occurs with the Sun, but remember you must never look at the Sun through binoculars or any telescope because of the danger of damaging your eyes.

**Points: 10**
See the Moon low on the horizon

**Points: 10**
See the Moon high in the sky

### VISIT A PLANETARIUM

**Points: 10** 10

A good way of learning about the sky is to visit a planetarium, where a special projector shows the night sky on the inside of a dome. At least there it is warm, so you can learn about the sky in comfort!

### LEARN STARS IN A PLANETARIUM

**Points: 10** 10

Planetariums have many different programmes about the planets, galaxies and black holes, for example. Try to attend a programme about how to find your way around the sky and learning the different constellations. With the naked eye you can see about 8500 stars over the whole sky.

**Points: 15**

Another good way of finding out which star can be seen, and at what times, is to use a planisphere. This is a special map of the sky, marked so that you can set it to any date and time. It then shows exactly what you will be able to see.

## BINOCULARS

**Points: 5**

You don't have to have a telescope to look at the night sky. You can see lots of things with just your eyes. If you can, borrow a pair of binoculars. They are often even better than big telescopes in helping you to see things in the sky and are easier to use.

**Points: 10**

## REFRACTING TELESCOPE

Amateur astronomers use various types of telescopes. One, known as a refractor, uses lenses at each end of a tube. (The large one where the light enters is known as the objective, and the smaller one, which is adjustable so everything looks sharp, is called the eyepiece.) You look straight through the telescope at the sky.

**Points: 10**

## REFLECTING TELESCOPE

Another type of telescope, known as a reflector, uses mirrors instead of lenses (as well as an eyepiece), and you have to look in the side of the tube. The mirrors act as a magnifier to enlarge the subject.

## SCHMIDT-CASSEGRAIN TELESCOPE

**Points: 15**

Some telescopes use both lenses and mirrors. They are popular with amateur astronomers because they are easy to carry from place to place. One type you may see is called a Schmidt-Cassegrain, named after two astronomers who designed telescopes.

## HOW THE SKY ROTATES

Although the stars are actually scattered about in space they look as if they are on the inside of a giant dome. When you stand outside – like the little figure in the diagram (below) – the stars are overhead and the horizon is all around you. Just as the Sun moves across the sky during the day, so the stars move during the night, because the Earth itself is rotating. One star, called Polaris, appears to stand still at the North Pole of the sky, and all the other stars seem to rotate around it. Only in a photograph, such as the one shown here (right), can you see that Polaris is not quite at the North Pole. The exposure needed for the photograph was several hours, and all the stars have left trails as the sky moved. The very short, bright trail near the centre was made by Polaris.

**15** Points: 15

*What is another name for Polaris?*

## FIND THE PLOUGH AND POLARIS

How do you find Polaris? First you find a well-known group of seven stars known as the Plough (or Dipper in North America), with an easily remembered shape, rather like a saucepan with a long handle. Because they are very close to the North Pole, the stars of the Plough never dip below the horizon. The two end stars of the Plough are called the Pointers, because a line through them points to Polaris.

Polaris

Pointers

*THE PLOUGH*

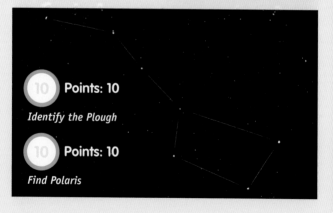

**10** **Points: 10**
*Identify the Plough*

**10** **Points: 10**
*Find Polaris*

## PICTURES IN THE SKY

Because the Earth revolves around the Sun once a year, the Sun appears to move slowly across the sky, hiding different stars during the daytime as the months go by. So the stars that you see at night also change with the time of the year. Later in this book you can see what the sky looks like during each of the four seasons. To help them find their way around the sky at different times of the year, earlier pioneers invented names for various groups of stars, or constellations. Astronomers use the Latin names for constellations in modern star atlases, so everyone, anywhere on Earth, knows which groups of stars they are talking about.

Cassiopeia

**Points: 10**
How many constellations cover the whole sky?

**Points: 10**
Old book of constellations

**Points: 10**
Modern star atlas

Most bright stars have individual names, and many of these come from Arabic words that described their positions in the imaginary constellation patterns on the sky. The red star at the top left of Orion, for example, is known as Betelgeuse, which probably means 'the woman in the middle' (the Arabs saw the constellation as a woman). The brilliant bluish star at the bottom right corner is Rigel, meaning 'foot'. The name Polaris in Ursa Major, however, comes from Latin.

**Points: 10**
What is the English name for Orion?

**Points: 10**
Book of constellations

**Points: 10**
Orion

Orion

Constellations close to Polaris (mainly those shown on the chart on page 25) always remain above the horizon. (They are known as 'circumpolar constellations'.) Many other constellations are farther away from Polaris and the North Pole, so they rise and set during the night. The diagram shows how the constellation called Orion (page 36) rises above the horizon in the east, becomes highest in the south, and then disappears as it sets in the west.

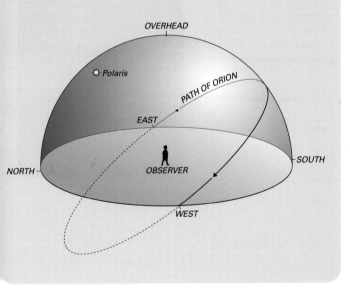

## WATCHING PLANETS

Stars shine because they are extremely hot and give out their own light. The Moon and planets, on the other hand, only reflect light from the Sun. Two planets, Venus and Jupiter, shine like very bright stars, and two others, Mars and Saturn, although fainter, are also sometimes easy to see. All these planets (and the other, fainter ones) orbit the Sun just like the Earth.

Venus and Jupiter with the Moon

**Points: 20**
Mars

**Points: 10**
Jupiter

**Points: 20**
Saturn (a yellowish colour)

**Points: 10**
Venus

## Points: 10

10
Who first saw Jupiter's satellites
through a telescope?

## JUPITER'S SATELLITES

Jupiter has four large satellites in orbit around it (three are
larger than our Moon). They are easily seen through binoculars,
appearing on each side of the planet.

**Points: 20** Jupiter's satellites

## MOVEMENT OF THE PLANETS

Because they are orbiting the Sun, planets do not have fixed
positions like the stars, so they cannot be drawn on the maps here.
You can sometimes find details of where they are in the newspapers
and also on the internet. Venus is always close to the Sun, so it is in
the west in the evening, and in the east early in the morning.

*There are several known dwarf planets, the largest of which is
Pluto (diameter 2374 kilometres). All except Ceres orbit in the
outermost Solar System.*

## THE PHASES OF THE MOON

As the Moon goes around the Earth, we see it by the light from the Sun that it reflects. It always turns the same side towards us, so sometimes it is in darkness, sometimes partly lit, and sometimes a complete, bright circle. At New Moon the disk is completely dark, but a very thin, young crescent that appears in the western sky shortly after sunset is often called by the same name. The ends of the crescent (the horns) are turned towards the east. As the days go by, the Moon appears farther towards the east at sunset, and the bright area waxes (increases). When half of the Moon can be seen, it is called First Quarter. The bright area continues to increase, until the whole face of the Moon is shining at Full Moon. Between First Quarter and Full Moon, the Moon is called waxing gibbous. After Full Moon the bright area begins to wane (decrease), first through waning gibbous, then Last Quarter, and finally to waning crescent, until it disappears close to the Sun in the east at sunrise.

**Points: 10**
Narrow crescent Moon
(New Moon)

**Points: 10**
The horns of the crescent

**Points: 10**
First Quarter

**Points: 10**
Waxing gibbous

**Points: 10**
Full Moon

**Points: 10**
Waning gibbous

**Points: 10**
Last Quarter

**Points: 10**
Waning crescent

axing phases

Full Moon

aning phases

17

## EARTHSHINE

Sometimes when the Moon appears as a crescent, you can see the rest of it, faintly illuminated by sunshine that has been reflected from the Earth on to the dark part of the Moon. This is called Earthshine.

**Points: 10**

## LUNAR SEAS AND HIGHLANDS

Some parts of the Moon's surface are darker than others. These dark grey areas are called maria (Latin for 'seas'). They are flat lava plains. Most of the Apollo missions to the Moon landed in the maria, because they were safer and more predictable than the more rugged areas. The lighter areas are called the highlands, and they contain nearly all the craters that pockmark the face of the Moon. One Apollo mission, Apollo 17, landed on the edge of the highlands. At Full Moon, some craters show bright rays where powdered rock has been splashed out by the impacts. The longest rays belong to a crater called Tycho.

**Points: 10**
Maria

**Points: 10**
Highlands

**Moon landings**
*Only six NASA space missions have
landed on the surface of the Moon:*

| | |
|---|---|
| Apollo 11 – 16 July 1969 | Apollo 15 – 26 July 1971 |
| Apollo 12 – 14 November 1969 | Apollo 16 – 16 April 1972 |
| Apollo 14 – 31 January 1971 | Apollo 17 – 7 December 1972 |

### ARTIFICIAL SATELLITES

As you watch the sky, especially at dawn and dusk, you will often see a slow-moving point of light crossing the sky. This is an artificial satellite, orbiting the Earth. Some, such as Iridium satellites, become very bright and then fade away.

### COMETS

You may be lucky enough to see a comet. Only rarely do these become bright enough for you to see them with the naked eye. A comet is a mixture of ice and dust – meteor dust comes from comets – and the heat of the Sun often makes it grow a long tail.

## METEORS

Sometimes you see a sudden, short streak of light. This is often called a 'shooting star', but its proper name is a meteor. (They are not stars, but tiny grains of dust that are burnt up as they dash through the Earth's atmosphere.) On a few nights of the year, the Earth passes through a cloud of dust, and we have a meteor shower, with dozens of meteors each hour. Very rarely, a meteor is brighter than any of the stars or planets; it is then called a fireball.

| | | |
|---|---|---|
| **Top Spot!** | **Points: 50** | Comet |
| **Top Spot!** | **Points: 50** | Fireball |
| | **Points: 30** | Meteor shower |
| | **Points: 10** | Meteor |
| | **Points: 10** | Artificial satellite |

*i* *Halley's Comet is the most famous comet. It returns every 76 years, most recently in 1986.*

21

## THE GREAT BEAR

It is best to start learning the sky with the Plough (page 8). It forms just part of the constellation of Ursa Major, the Great Bear. The picture shows how the constellation used to be drawn on old maps of the sky. The two end stars are called the Pointers, because a line through them points to Polaris (page 8), the star that stands still. The Pointers are called Dubhe and Merak.

**Points: 5**
Ursa Major

**Points: 10**
Dubhe

**Points: 10**
Merak

**Points: 10**
Why do the Great and Little Bear appear odd in all old constellation drawings?

## THE LITTLE BEAR

Polaris is the brightest star in Ursa Minor, the Little Bear (see page 22). The two stars closest to Ursa Major are known as The Guards, and one, Kochab, is quite bright. The diagram shows how the two constellations appear to swing round the North Pole (and Polaris) during the course of the night.

URSA MINOR
Polaris
Guards   Kochab
URSA MAJOR   Dubhe
Merak
NORTH

**5** Points: 5
Ursa Minor

**10** Points: 10
The Guards

**10** Points: 10
Kochab

# CONSTELLATIONS NEAR THE NORTH POLE

## CASSIOPEIA

There are several other constellations near the North Pole. If you find the star called Megrez, where Ursa Major's 'tail' joins the body, and imagine a line from there to Polaris and beyond, you come to a group of five stars in the shape of a 'W' – or an 'M' when they are the other way up! These form the constellation of Cassiopeia (page 25), an ancient, legendary queen.

## DRACO

Snaking its way around the pole is a long, faint constellation called Draco, the Dragon. At the end of its long, winding 'body', four stars make up its lozenge-shaped 'head'. The middle star of the three that form Ursa Major's 'tail' is Mizar. Between Mizar and the Guards is Thuban in Draco.

## CEPHEUS

Between the head of Draco and Cassiopeia is the constellation of Cepheus (page 39), a legendary king, husband of Cassiopeia. The stars in this constellation form a pointed shape like the gable end of a house.

**Points: 10**
Cassiopeia

**Points: 10**
Draco

CASSIOPEIA

**Points: 10**
What is strange about Mizar (look at it through binoculars if you are not sure)?

CEPHEUS

Polaris

URSA MINOR

Kochab

Dubhe

Merak

Thuban

Megrez

Phecda

Alioth

Mizar

DRACO

URSA MAJOR

Alkaid

**Points: 10**
Cepheus

**Points: 10**
Mizar

**Points: 10**
Megrez

**Points: 10**
Thuban

## ANDROMEDA, PEGASUS AND PERSEUS

Do you know the Greek legend of how Andromeda, the daughter of Cassiopeia and Cepheus, came to be chained to a rock, and was about to be killed by the terrible sea monster Cetus (see map page 48)? She was rescued just in time by Perseus, who had earlier killed the dreadful Gorgon, Medusa. Medusa's head, with snakes for hair, turned anyone who looked at it to stone. Perseus was clever and only viewed her reflection. He showed the head to Cetus, who became a rock. After rescuing Andromeda, Perseus and Andromeda rode away on Pegasus, the flying horse (which appears upside down in the sky). You can find all these legendary beings in the sky (see the maps on pages 38 and 48, for example). The old constellation drawing of Perseus shows him holding Medusa's head. This is represented in the sky by the star Algol, whose name comes from the Arabic words Al Guhl, meaning 'the demon'. The photograph shows the constellation pattern and a bright comet, Comet Hyakutake.

**Points: 10**
Pegasus

**Points: 10**
Cetus

Andromeda and Pegasus

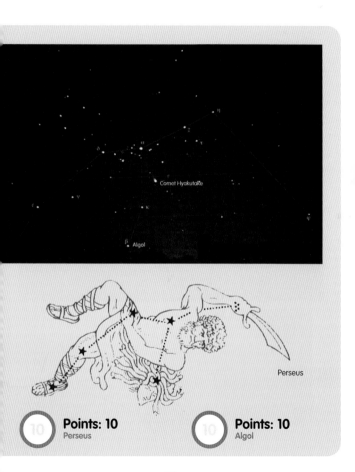

Comet Hyakutake

Algol

Perseus

**Points: 10**
Perseus

**Points: 10**
Algol

**Points: 10**
Summer Triangle

High in the sky in the middle of summer is the Summer Triangle, the corners of which are formed by the very bright stars of Deneb in Cygnus, the Swan; Vega in Lyra, the Lyre; and Altair in Aquila, the Eagle.

**Points: 10**
Aquila

**Points: 10**
Cygnus

**Points: 10**
Lyra

### CYGNUS

Cygnus is sometimes known as the 'Northern Cross' and the name Deneb means 'the tail' in Arabic because it marks the tail of the Swan. The bright star at the other end (the 'beak') of the constellation is Albireo, but its name has no real meaning, because it arose after a series of errors and bad translations.

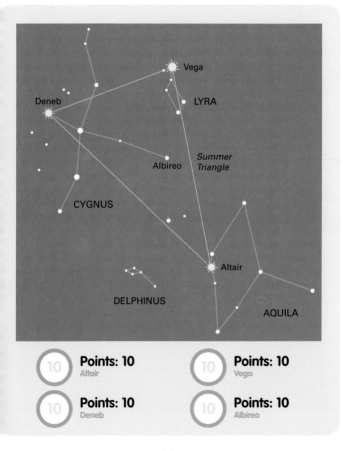

## THE MILKY WAY

**Points: 10**

The Milky Way is a silvery band of light that stretches right across the sky and is easiest to see in summer. The faint light comes from hundreds of thousands of stars which are so closely crowded together that you cannot see them as individual stars. With binoculars you can see that there appears no limit to the number of stars in the Milky Way, which is actually our edge-on view of the main disk of the Galaxy in which we live, and which contains over one hundred thousand million stars.

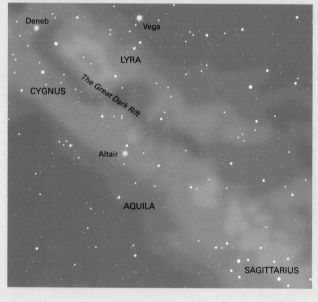

## GREAT DARK RIFT

**Points: 20**

The densest part of the northern Milky Way runs from Cygnus down towards Sagittarius (page 45). Cygnus appears to be flying down the Milky Way. Can you see the Great Dark Rift in Cygnus? This may look like a 'hole in the stars', but actually there are just as many there as elsewhere in the Milky Way, but most are hidden by dark clouds of dust between the stars.

> *Black holes are completely invisible, because not even light can escape from them, but they can be detected by their effects on nearby stars. The closest known black hole is orbiting a faint star in Cygnus.*

The Milky Way

## OPEN CLUSTERS

**Points: 10**
Pleiades

10

Inside our own Galaxy stars are born in groups (known as clusters) from the material between the stars. Those with young, blue stars are known as open clusters, and usually contain a few tens of stars which are only a few million years old. The most famous open cluster is the Pleiades, in Taurus (see page 39). Other open clusters are older, such as the Double Cluster in Perseus (see map on page 42), which can be seen through binoculars.

Pleiades

32

**Points: 15**
M13, in Hercules

### GLOBULAR CLUSTERS

There are other clusters that are much older, at least ten thousand million years old. These are the globular clusters, which are spherical in shape and each contain many thousands of stars. The most famous in the northern sky is M13, in Hercules (see map page 50).

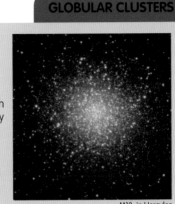

M13, in Hercules

### NEBULAE

**Points: 20**
Orion Nebula

A cloud of gas between the stars is known as a nebula (plural 'nebulae'), but only one, the great Orion Nebula (page 36), is easily visible to the naked eye.

Orion Nebula

### THE SEASONAL CHARTS

The charts on the following pages show the sky during the four different seasons of the year. There are two charts for each season, one looking east, the other looking west.

AQUARIUS

PEGASUS

DELPHINUS

Altair

CYGNUS

CE

AQUILA

Albireo

Deneb

LYRA  Vega

HERCULES

DRACO

OPHIUCHUS

CORONA
BOREALIS

Gemma

BOÖTES

Arcturus

VIRGO

Spica

*i* Astronomers measure distances between the stars in light years – the time it takes for light to travel from stars to us. Light travels at nearly 300,000 kilometres per second.

## STARS AROUND THE NORTH POLE

This chart shows all the stars that you can see if you live in the Northern Hemisphere. With it you can find your way from one constellation to another. The North Pole of the sky and Polaris are in the centre.

CETUS
SCES
Mira
OMEDA Hamal
ARIES
TAURUS
TRIANGULUM
Algol *Pleiades*
PERSEUS Aldebaran Rigel
EIA
Capella
Betelgeuse ORION
AURIGA
Castor GEMINI
Pollux
MAJOR
Procyon
CANIS MINOR
CANCER
LEO
Regulus HYDRA
bola
Alphard

Light from Sirius (see next page), the brightest star in the sky, takes 8.6 years to reach the Earth.

35

## WINTER – LOOKING EAST

Winter is the best time to see Orion and the stars of Canis Major and Canis Minor, the Greater and Lesser Dogs. Betelgeuse, in Orion, is a gigantic type of star, called a red supergiant. If it were in the Solar System in place of the Sun, the Earth would be below its surface. Its colour is in sharp contrast to bluish-white Rigel on the other side of the constellation. Sirius, in Canis Major, is the brightest star in the sky. Venus and Jupiter, which are planets (page 14), are the only objects that ever appear brighter.

**Points: 10**
What is another name for Sirius?

The Orion Nebula is a vast cloud of gas and dust, just visible to the naked eye as a fuzzy spot below Orion's belt. Dozens of new stars are being created within it.

**Points: 15**
The stars of Orion's bel

**Points: 10**
Betelgeuse

## WINTER – LOOKING WEST

Altair, one of the Summer Triangle (page 28) will have disappeared, but Vega can still be seen low on the horizon in the north-west, while Deneb is higher up in the same part of the sky. Andromeda, with its great galaxy (page 49) and the small neighbouring constellations of Triangulum, the Triangle, and Aries, the Ram, with one bright star, Hamal, are still easy to see. High in the south is the constellation of Perseus, and lower down, Taurus, the Bull, whose 'eye' is orange Aldebaran. Taurus contains two clusters, the Pleiades (page 32) and the 'V' of stars near Aldebaran, known as the Hyades.

**Points: 20**
Double Cluster

**Points: 15**
Hyades

**Points: 10**
Aldebaran

PERSEUS

Algol

Double
Cluster

CASSIOPEIA

Polaris

URSA
MINOR

URSA
MAJOR

TRIANGULUM

Hamal

M31

ARIES

ANDROMEDA

CEPHEUS

DRACO

HERCULES

Deneb

Vega

PEGASUS

CYGNUS

LYRA

NORTH

WEST

| 10 | **Points: 10**<br>Hamal | 10 | **Points: 10**<br>Taurus |
|----|----|----|----|
| 10 | **Points: 10**<br>Aries | 10 | **Points: 10**<br>Triangulum |

## SPRING – LOOKING EAST

If you follow the line of the Pointers, not towards Polaris, but in the opposite direction, you come to the great constellation of Leo, the Lion. The 'backward question mark' of stars (with Regulus as the 'dot') forming the lion's head (see the next chart on page 42) is known as The Sickle. At the other end of Leo, Denebola forms the 'tail' of the lion. You can follow the curve of the tail of Ursa Major, or a line from Regulus to Denebola, to help you find Arcturus, the brightest star in Boötes, the Herdsman. Low on the horizon are the four stars of Corvus, the Crow.

| | Points: 10 | | Points: 10 |
|---|---|---|---|
| 10 | Arcturus | 10 | Corvus |
| 10 | Points: 10 | 10 | Points: 10 |
| | Boötes | | Denebola |

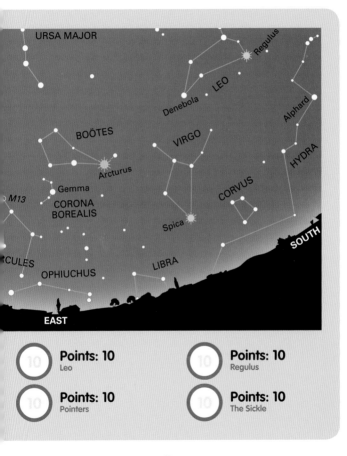

URSA MAJOR
Regulus
LEO
Denebola
Alphard
BOÖTES
VIRGO
HYDRA
Arcturus
Gemma
M13
CORONA
BOREALIS
CORVUS
Spica
SOUTH
CULES
OPHIUCHUS
LIBRA
EAST

| | |
|---|---|
| **Points: 10** Leo | **Points: 10** Regulus |
| **Points: 10** Pointers | **Points: 10** The Sickle |

## SPRING – LOOKING WEST

Spring is a good time to see the constellation of Gemini, the Twins, which consists of two, almost parallel lines of stars, running west from the two bright stars Castor and Pollux. Between Leo and Gemini is the faint constellation of Cancer, the Crab. Below Gemini is the small constellation of Canis Minor, the Lesser Dog, with just one bright star, Procyon. High in the north-west is the constellation of Auriga, the Charioteer. In old drawings he is shown carrying two young goats in his arms, so the little triangle of stars to the right of bright Capella is known as The Kids.

**Points: 15**
The Kids

**Points: 10**
Auriga

**Points: 10**
Cancer

**Points: 10**
Capella

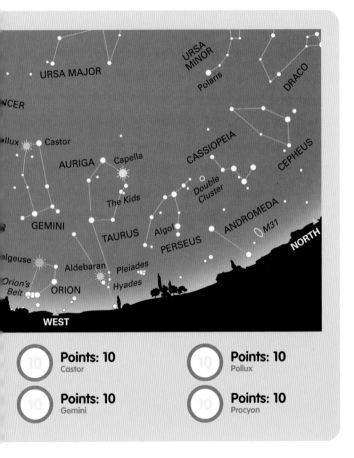

URSA MAJOR

URSA MINOR

Polaris

DRACO

NCER

llux   Castor

AURIGA   Capella

CASSIOPEIA

CEPHEUS

The Kids

Double Cluster

GEMINI

TAURUS   Algol

ANDROMEDA   M31

NORTH

elgeuse   Aldebaran   Pleiades

PERSEUS

Orion's Belt   ORION   Hyades

WEST

**Points: 10**
Castor

**Points: 10**
Pollux

**Points: 10**
Gemini

**Points: 10**
Procyon

43

## SUMMER – LOOKING EAST

Although it does not get dark until very late and the nights are short, summer is the best time to see the great Summer Triangle (page 28) and the star clouds of the Milky Way, which consist of thousands and thousands of stars, too close together to be seen as separate points of light. Very low in the south is Sagittarius, the Archer. Can you spy the 'Teapot' among its stars? To the east is the fainter constellation of Capricornus, the Sea-Goat, and the rather brighter one of Aquarius, the Water Carrier. Between them and Cygnus lies the tiny constellation of Delphinus, the Dolphin.

Aquila

**Points: 20**
'Teapot'

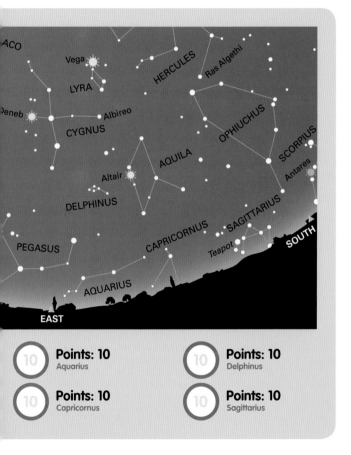

## SUMMER – LOOKING WEST

If you follow the curve of the tail of the Plough (as described on page 41) and go beyond Arcturus, you come to Spica, the brightest star in the constellation of Virgo, the Virgin. East of Boötes is the semicircle of stars of the constellation of Corona Borealis, the Northern Crown. The brightest star is called Gemma, the Jewel. To the east lies the large constellation of Ophiuchus, the Serpent Bearer. Below this is Scorpius, the Scorpion. Its brightest star is Antares, the 'Rival of Mars', so called because, like the planet, it is deep red in colour. Between Antares and Spica lies the constellation of Libra, the Balance (or Scales).

 Points: 10
Antares

Points: 10
Corona Borealis

 Points: 10
Gemma

Points: 10
Libra

46

DRACO

URSA MINOR

Polaris

CEPHEUS

CASSIOPEIA

Double Cluster

PERSEUS

BOÖTES

Arcturus

URSA MAJOR

Capella

Denebola

AURIGA

NORTH

CANCER

Castor

LEO

Regulus

WEST

| | **Points: 10**<br>Ophiuchus | | **Points: 10**<br>Spica |
|---|---|---|---|
| | **Points: 10**<br>Scorpius | | **Points: 10**<br>Virgo |

## AUTUMN – LOOKING EAST

Rising high in the east is the Great Square of Pegasus. The star at the north-eastern corner actually belongs to Andromeda. Part of the way along the line of four bright stars in Andromeda, two more point at right angles to the north, indicating the position of the Great Andromeda Galaxy (also known as M31). It needs to be very clear and dark for you to see this galaxy. Just think, the light you see started its journey at about the time when the first humans began to evolve from ape-like creatures! Below Pegasus lies the faint constellation of Pisces, the Fishes, and still farther south, there is the large area of sky known as Cetus, the Sea Monster. Unfortunately many of the stars in this area are rather faint. If you are lucky, however you may just be able to see, very, very low in the south, Fomalhaut in Piscis Austrinus, the Southern Fish.

**Points: 20**
The Great Andromeda G

**Points: 15**
Great Square of Pegasus

48

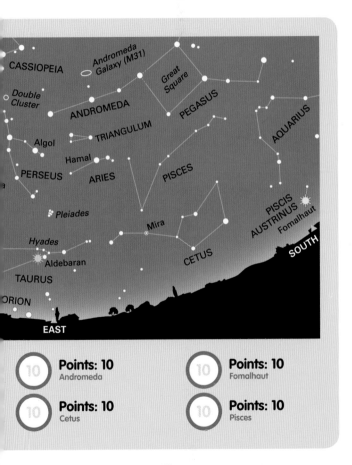

CASSIOPEIA

Andromeda
Galaxy (M31)

Great
Square

Double
Cluster

ANDROMEDA

PEGASUS

AQUARIUS

Algol

TRIANGULUM

Hamal

PISCES

PERSEUS

ARIES

PISCIS
AUSTRINUS
Fomalhaut

Pleiades

Mira

SOUTH

Hyades

Aldebaran

CETUS

TAURUS

ORION

EAST

| | Points: 10 | | Points: 10 |
|---|---|---|---|
| 10 | Andromeda | 10 | Fomalhaut |
| 10 | Points: 10 | 10 | Points: 10 |
| | Cetus | | Pisces |

## AUTUMN – LOOKING WEST

Like the constellations of Andromeda and Pegasus, Hercules, the legendary hero, is upside down! One foot rests on Draco in the north. The name of one star Ras Algethi, means 'the kneeling man's head' in Arabic. The main part of the body is known as the 'Keystone' because the arrangement of the four stars is just like the shape of the central stone in an archway. On the western side of the Keystone lies the globular cluster, M13 (see page 33). It is still possible to see most of the Summer Triangle and the bright stars of Vega, Deneb and Altair (see page 28), as well as much of the Milky Way which also runs through the constellations of Cassiopeia and Perseus.

**Points: 10**
How many labours did Hercules have to accomplish?

**Points: 20**
The cluster M13

Deneb

CEPHEUS

Polaris

URSA MINOR

CYGNUS

HINUS

Albireo

Vega

LYRA

HERCULES

DRACO

M13

URSA MAJOR

UILA

Ras
Algethi

CORONA
BOREALIS

NORTH

Gemma

BOÖTES

OPHIUCHUS

WEST

**Points: 10**
Ras Algethi

**Points: 10**
Hercules

## HOW DO SOLAR ECLIPSES HAPPEN?

Although it does not happen at night, the Moon sometimes comes between the Sun and the Earth (at New Moon), similar to the way lunar eclipses occur. The Sun and Moon appear almost exactly the same size in the sky, and the Moon blocks out the sunlight to give a solar eclipse. This is a sight not to be missed if you have the chance.

Top Spot!  Points: 50

## TOTAL SOLAR ECLIPSES

Along a very narrow line on the surface of the Earth, the Sun may be completely hidden by the Moon, in a total solar eclipse, generally for no more than about 3–4 minutes. The way the shadow sweeps across the Earth is very dramatic, and during totality the beautiful outer atmosphere of the Sun, the corona, becomes visible.

← Progression of eclipse

*i* You must NEVER look at the Sun through binoculars or a telescope, because it would damage your eyes or even blind you.

*i* It takes light about eight minutes to reach us from the Sun, but about four years to travel to the nearest star (which is called Proxima Centauri).

## Points: 20

## PARTIAL SOLAR ECLIPSES

The Moon only throws a tiny shadow on the surface of the Earth, so you are much less likely to see a solar eclipse than a lunar one. You are most likely to see a partial solar eclipse, when the Moon hides just part of the Sun.

## ANNULAR SOLAR ECLIPSES

## Points: 40

Because the distances to the Moon and Sun change, sometimes the Moon does not completely cover the disk of the Sun, and a ring of light remains visible, in an annular eclipse. Although only visible from a narrow path on the Earth, they can last for about 12 minutes, and are slightly more common than total eclipses.

## NACREOUS CLOUDS

**Points: 30**

Rarely, shortly after sunset (or before sunrise, if you are up that early), you may see clouds with beautiful bands of different colours. These are nacreous (mother-of-pearl) clouds made of ice particles. They are so high (15–30km) that they are illuminated by the Sun, even though the ground is in darkness.

**Points: 30**

## NOCTILUCENT CLOUDS

Occasionally, during the summer months of late May, June and July, bluish-white, wispy clouds may be seen in the north, around midnight. These are noctilucent ('night-shining') clouds, the highest of all at about 80km above the ground. They are also made of ice, and reflect light from the Sun that is hidden far below the northern horizon.

**Points: 30**

Quite frequently, the Sun sends out streams of charged (that is, electrified) particles. When these hit the Earth's atmosphere, they cause the air to glow, giving an aurora: changing patterns of light high in the sky.

## OBSERVATORY

You may be lucky enough to visit an observatory, which is where professional astronomers study the stars. They often have several telescopes, which are usually very large reflectors (page 7). Do not expect to look through one, though! The telescopes are only used with highly complicated digital cameras and other equipment. But many observatories have visitor centres that you can visit.

**Points: 10**
Observatory

**Points: 10**
Observatory visitor centre

**Points: 10**
A great telescope

Royal Greenwich Observatory

## AMATEUR OBSERVATORY

Many local amateur astronomical societies have observatories, and these often hold open days where you can visit and may be able to look through some of the telescopes. Like professional observatories, the telescopes are usually protected by a dome.

**Points: 10**
Amateur observatory

**Points: 10**
Dome

**Points: 10**
Look through a telescope

## RADIO OBSERVATORY

Nowadays, astronomy is carried out in many different ways: with radio telescopes (with both large dishes and 'TV-type' aerials), and with satellites. Again, some radio observatories have visitor centres, and you can see typical satellites at some space centres.

**Points: 20**
Radio observatory visitor centre

**Points: 10**
Radio observatory

**Points: 10**
Dish telescope

Jodrell Bank Observatory

## A VOYAGE OF DISCOVERY

You can learn a lot about astronomy by visiting a museum. Some are in old observatories. There you will often find displays explaining about planets, stars, galaxies, and other strange things like black holes! But you can also see many of the old instruments that earlier astonomers used.

## CELESTIAL GLOBE

One of the simplest devices is a celestial globe which shows the stars, usually with the old constellation drawings.

Points: 10

## ASTROLABE

A more complicated device is an astrolabe, which is a special form of sky map. A planisphere (page 5) is a simplified modern version.

Points: 10

### ARMILLARY SPHERE

You may also see an armillary sphere, which is a collection of rings that may be used to show the movements of the Sun, Moon and stars in the sky.

 Points: 10

### ORRERY

Sometimes you may see an orrery, which is a working model of the Solar System where the planets move at correct relative speeds around the Sun.

Points: 10

### METEORITE

Points: 10

Occasionally some meteors (page 21) are large enough to land on Earth. They are very old indeed, and tell scientists who study them about the time when the Sun and planets themselves were formed.

# INDEX

**Answers: P9** Polaris – Pole Star; **P11** Constellations – 88; **P12** Orion – The Hunter; **P15** Jupiter – Galileo; **P22** Great and Little Bears – the Bears have tails; **P25** Mizar – it is a double star; **P36** Sirius – Dog Star; **P50** Hercules – 12 Labours;

# i-SPY

## How to get your i-SPY certificate and badge

Let us know when you've become a super-spotter with 1000 points and we'll send you a special certificate and badge!

## HERE'S WHAT TO DO!

 Ask an adult to check your score.

Visit www.collins.co.uk/i-SPY to apply for your certificate. If you are under the age of 13 you will need a parent or guardian to do this.

We'll send your certificate via email and you'll receive a brilliant badge through the post!